Not Only the Su **Protect Their Money from Litigation**

The Ultimate Guide to Asset Preservation

Josh Bennett
Attorney at Law

The Ultimate Guide to Asset Preservation
Not Only the Super-Rich Need to Protect Their Money from Litigation

Visit us on the Web at www.BGPublishingInternational.com

Published by BG Publishing International
1304 SW 160th Avenue, Suite 203, Sunrise FL 33326

Cover and Page Design by Perseus Design

ISBN 978-1-936738-02-1

To my lovely wife, Caren, and our children, Marti and Sam, for all your love and support throughout the years, I lovingly dedicate this book.

Also, to my parents, Martin and Gloria, my love and heartfelt thanks for teaching me what is truly important in life.

Table of Contents

Chapter One Asset Preservation Planning................................7

Chapter Two Offshore Planning.................................. 19

Chapter Three Does Situs Matter? 31

Chapter Four Why a Directed Trust? 49

Chapter Five Other Techniques to Consider 53

Chapter Six Who Benefits Most from

Asset Preservation Planning?.......................... 61

Chapter Seven Frequently Asked Questions............................ 69

Glossary.. 79

Index 85

CHAPTER 1

Asset Preservation Planning

It is an unfortunate human failing that a full pocketbook often groans more loudly than an empty stomach. ~Franklin Delano Roosevelt

The best time to engage in asset protection planning in not after you have accumulated wealth, but when you **decide** to accumulate it. This will become abundantly clear as you read through this book. You will, as President Roosevelt so aptly puts it, face more and more threats to your wealth the larger it becomes — and taxes are only the most obvious menace.

Why do I need to protect my assets?

Ask yourself these questions:

- Are you in a **high-risk business**, such as medicine or accounting?

Yes, believe it or not, accounting is a high risk business. A recent paper on auditor liability reported that industry estimates for the accounting profession revealed a whopping 4,000 lawsuits for a total of $30 billion in potential liability.

The landscape is even grimmer for doctors. According to a study done by the American Medical Association during 2007 and 2008, for every ten doctors 55 and older, six have been sued. Male physicians are two times as likely to be sued as female physicians. The type of medicine you practice can also have an effect. In addition, and this is key in asset protection, if you have an ownership interest in your medical practice, you have a greater likelihood of getting sued. In the AMA report, 47.5% of physicians with such interests were sued, whereas 33.4% of those with no ownership interest were sued.

According to the Physician Insurers Association of America, most of these suits never make it to court. Of the lawsuits that were reported in the AMA study, 65% were dropped (at an estimated cost of $22,163 for those who had to be defended to some degree), approximately 25% were settled, 4.5% were resolved by some form of alternative dispute resolution, and 5% actually went to trial. Of that 5%, the doctors won 90% of all cases, but at a cost of more than $100,000 per case!

Worse, if you are part of the 10% who lose, you could become liable for an enormous sum. Fifty-two percent of all malpractice awards were in excess of $1 million as of 2005 and the average jury award was $4.7 million! And that's just the average.

Could your personal assets withstand such an attack?

It does not take being in a high risk profession either. Anyone can be the victim of a **frivolous or predatory lawsuit.** All it takes is someone knowing that you have money. Suddenly, that someone claims to have slipped and fallen in your apartment building; or, you are accused of sexual harassment by one of your employees. The list goes on.

Again, can you afford to defend against a hungry plaintiff's attorney who is working for a piece of the recovery? Such attorneys typically work on a contingent fee basis and receive between 25 to 33.3 percent (if the case is settled) and 33 to 40 percent if the case goes to trial.

- What if you were faced with **personal bankruptcy?**

Would you be able to walk away with most of your assets intact?

Certain exemptions provide limited protection from creditor attack and that includes bankruptcies. One of these is the **Homestead Exemption.** Under this exemption, some or all of the equity in your home is not reachable by creditors. The amount of this exemption varies by state. In Florida, it is unlimited. However, what of your other assets?

Are your trademarks and trade name secure if you have to start over with your business?

If they aren't separated from your operating company, chances are they are not secure.

- Is your retirement plan secure?

Can creditors reach into your plan and deprive you of your retirement savings?

All so-called "ERISA qualified" plans are fully protected under federal law and not reachable by creditors. These are 401(k)s and the like. IRAs and ROTH IRAs are not ERISA qualified and therefore do not enjoy such protection. However, some states, like Florida, will protect your retirement accounts from creditor attack. Other states will do a balancing test between the needs of the debtor and the rights of the creditor.

- What if you were in an accident today and it was your fault?

Would your personal assets be safe from attack?

You have liability insurance to cover you in case of this very nightmare. But, what if it was a very bad accident and the jury awarded punitive damages against you? Will your liability insurer pay those costs? Or, will you be left with an astronomical verdict against your personal assets? What if you simply do not have enough coverage?

One judgment, rightly or wrongly entered against you, could wipe you out at any time if you haven't planned ahead to protect your assets.

- What if you were to incur unexpected medical bills?

Even people with extensive medical insurance coverage sometimes experience unexpected catastrophic medical issues or emergencies. The cost of these bills can mount quickly, suddenly resulting in more medical bills than most people accumulate over a lifetime.

What is it that I need to protect?

- *My home*
- *My estate for my beneficiaries*
- *My retirement*
- *My businesses*
- *My real estate*
- *My investments*
- *Trade names and other intellectual property*
- *My hard-earned wealth*

Your home is only safe to the extent of the homestead exemption that exists in your state. Beyond that, a creditor can force a foreclosure and take the remaining equity.

If your retirement plan is not an ERISA qualified plan, or if your state does not specifically exempt it, your retirement plan is not exempt from creditor attack. In that case, a creditor can potentially reach into your plan and take all that you have accumulated.

You must not underestimate the vulnerability of your business. Common stock that you own in your professional corporation is subject to creditor attack at any time.

Furthermore, retail and other businesses, such as apartment houses, are ripe for lawsuits involving slips and falls and similar allegations.

If you were to suffer a bankruptcy in your business today, you would lose not only your business, but also the good name and all of the goodwill that you have worked so hard to build and protect.

What can I do to protect my assets?

The simplest form of asset protection is insurance. Make sure you have comprehensive liability policies on all of your risks: cars, houses, businesses. You might also consider an umbrella policy. It can give you an added layer of protection. Next, you will need to determine what level of protection you require. There is a wide variety of asset protection steps you can take.

For our purposes, however, we will concentrate on certain structures that either *put your assets beyond the reach of creditors, or make it so expensive, difficult, and frustrating for creditors to come after your assets that they will either give up or be much more likely to settle reasonably.* This is the purpose of asset protection planning.

The single most important thing to remember when planning to protect your assets is to do so BEFORE any claims or lawsuits arise. You must transfer your assets into an asset protection structure before anyone can claim any right to them. If you don't, you may well run afoul of one or more *fraudulent transfer* rules.

The second most important thing to remember is that it is rarely too late to protect your assets.

To protect the assets we've already identified, we could use any or all of the following structures. Understand that these are just some of the most common and widely used techniques, but by no means should this be considered an exhaustive list. Each technique or structure has different features, different tax consequences and different legal characteristics. Finding the right combination depends upon many things, including what business you're in and what will provide you the most beneficial tax situation.

- Corporation (C or S)
- Limited Partnership (LP)
- Family Limited Partnership (FLP)
- Limited Liability Company (LLC)
- Domestic Asset Protection Trust (DAPT)
- International Business Corporation (IBC)
- Offshore Asset Protection Trust (OAPT)

We will concentrate on the Asset Protection Trust (APT) and the Limited Liability Company (LLC), as they are by far the superior vehicles.

What are Asset Protection Trusts and what can they do?

First, let's establish precisely what a trust is and what it isn't. A trust is simply a contract between the **grantor** (also called the **settlor**), and the **trustee** that you appoint to take certain actions on behalf of one or more **beneficiaries**. Here, the trustee takes legal title to the assets, but equitable title is in the beneficiaries. Ideally, you will be the beneficiary, perhaps the only beneficiary. The grantor can be an individual, including you, or another legal entity such as a corporation. The trustee could be a person or an institution, and the beneficiary could be you, one or more other persons, or other legal entity as well.

The trust, as a legal entity, can act much like a person. It can own, buy, sell, borrow, lend, and form its own contracts.

In order to create an effective asset protection trust, this contract must be **irrevocable,** meaning you relinquish to the trustee all your rights to the trust's assets without allowing yourself any right to take the trust assets back or amend the trust. Furthermore, you need to make it a spendthrift trust. This means that, where a beneficiary has pledged his expectancy in the trust to a creditor, the trustee will ignore the creditor's claim. This "spendthrift clause" was originally meant to protect fools from being parted from their money. Now it protects you from your creditors.

To be truly effective, all distributions from the trust should be discretionary with the trustee. This is important from an asset protection standpoint in that, if there are no pending or expected distributions to point to, then you or your beneficiaries have no discernable income from the trust to attach.

Once you have set up your trust, you fund it with some or all of the assets you wish to protect. Remember that the trust may not be the only structure you are using to protect yourself, but it is by far one of the most powerful. This is simply because of this split ownership between you and the trustee. If you don't own an asset, it can't be used to pay a creditor. This is also why planning ahead so as not to run afoul of the fraudulent transfer rules is so important.

- *Self-Settled Trusts:* A self-settled trust is a trust you establish with yourself as the beneficiary. Alaska, Delaware, and Nevada were the first to enact anti-creditor trust acts allowing these self-settled spendthrift trusts. Other states have followed, including South Dakota. These states have enacted legislation that not only allows self-settled spendthrift trusts, but also shortens the statute of limitations for a creditor to challenge a transfer to such a trust. South Dakota's statute is only three years. Finally, they have made it more difficult for a creditor to prove fraudulent transfers into these trusts. Trusts settled in these jurisdictions are sometimes called **domestic asset protection trusts** or **DAPTs**. There has been criticism of the DAPT as an asset protection tool, stemming mainly from the fact that no one knows whether the other states will uphold the laws of Alaska, Delaware, Nevada or South Dakota if the trust assets aren't actually situated within those states. As of January 2010, it had not been tested.

One way around the issue of the self-settled trust is to make an LLC or other entity the legal beneficiary of the trust. Thus, by definition it would no longer be self-settled. But use caution in choosing such an entity, because, if you can be considered the beneficial owner of that entity, you could be right back where you started.

What can't an Asset Protection Trust do?

Generally, an asset protection trust cannot save you from being taxed. It will also not truly hide your assets. And, if your assets are derived from fraud or other criminal activity, you may not enjoy the benefits of the AP trust. Then again, you may, if you don't mind spending six months in jail for contempt. Michael and Denyse Anderson were convicted for their involvement in a famous Ponzi scheme that scammed people out of millions of dollars. Some of this money was hidden away by the Andersons in a trust in the Cook Islands. The Andersons had even made **themselves** co-trustees. But, when the U.S. court ordered the funds repatriated, the Andersons failed to comply. The judge found them in contempt and put them in jail. Eventually, they were released and settled with the Federal Trade Commission for pennies on the dollar. So, even though they held funds derived from fraud and criminal activity, they got to keep them, despite the fact that they set their trust up incorrectly.

Of course, no one is suggesting that you take such a course of action. This was merely an extreme illustration of the strength of these asset protection trusts. Furthermore, you wouldn't want to spend time in jail for failure to comply with a court order. Asset protection trusts work, especially when set up properly and BEFORE any claims arise. Let's talk about the timing of asset transfers and what that could mean for your asset protection trust.

How can creditors get at my assets?

Fraudulent Transfer Rules: It cannot be emphasized enough the importance of planning early and getting your asset protection (AP) plan in place before you have any judgments or other claims against your assets. Realize that the longer your asset sits in your AP structure, whether it is a trust, LLC, or otherwise, the less likely it is that a creditor will convince a judge to set aside or nullify your transfer of that asset into that AP structure.

Each state has its own fraudulent transfer rules in addition to those contained in the federal Bankruptcy Code, the Uniform Fraudulent Conveyances Act (UFCA) and the Uniform Fraudulent Transfers Act (UFTA). There are two types of transfers for the purposes of these rules: those made with **actual intent** to hinder, delay, or defraud any creditor, and those involving **constructive fraud**.

- Actual Intent: Actual intent must be shown through circumstantial evidence. Each state and the UFCA and UFTA have numerous "badges of fraud," points that demonstrate that a transfer was made with the actual intent to hinder, delay, or defraud any creditor. Some of those badges are:

- Did the debtor transfer to an insider?
- Did the debtor retain possession of or control over the asset after the transfer?
- Was the transfer concealed versus disclosed?
- Did the debtor transfer substantially all of his assets?
- Did the debtor remove or conceal assets?
- After transferring the assets, did the debtor run away?

Here, however, the debtor is allowed to show other non-fraudulent reasons for the transfer.

The two most important badges are:

- Did the debtor transfer the asset when insolvent?
- Did the debtor transfer the asset for less than fair market value?

- *Constructive Fraud:* While actual intent is a subjective test, constructive fraud is a more objective endeavor. Here, the judge just looks at the numbers. Again, he looks at:
  - Was the asset transferred for less than fair market value?
  - Was the debtor insolvent at the time of the transfer?

If you are solvent at the time of the transfer in question, it will defeat constructive fraud and most of the principal badges of fraud as well.

The statute of limitations for fraudulent transfers is generally around four years, although it varies by state. South Dakota, for instance, has a three-year statute. In some foreign jurisdictions, the statutes can be as short as one year or even less. The bottom line is that, the longer your asset has been sitting in your asset protection structure, the better your position will be with the court.

It is important to note that, for bankruptcy purposes, the court looks back ten (10) years before the filing of the petition to assess if the transfer was made to a **self-settled trust,** and whether the transfer was made with **actual intent** to hinder, delay, or defraud any entity to which the debtor was or became indebted, either on or after the date that the transfer was made.

What are the actual consequences of fraudulent transfer?

Recovering the transferred asset is the remedy for fraudulent transfer. In this case, a judge may order you to return the asset, or "repatriate" it if it is held in a foreign trust. However, if you do not own the asset anymore (since it is in trust), and have no control over it, you may not be able to comply. There has been more than one case where a judge has put debtors in jail for failure to repatriate assets. Michael and Denyse Anderson, who helped steal those millions in a Ponzi scheme, were incarcerated because they were co-trustees of their Cook Islands trust and arguably had control. They were eventually set free when the judge came to understand that the assets were out of their immediate reach due to a duress clause. It's startling how this all turned out, considering that the Andersons had made a fatal error in setting up their asset protection trust: they had made themselves trustees with the right to distribute the funds!

But, the fact is, there is precedent for debtors going to jail for failing to return assets to pay creditors. Stephen J. Lawrence was also jailed in August 2000 for failure to repatriate funds from his Mauritius trust. His incarceration was affirmed by the 11th Circuit Court of Appeals and his Writ of

Certiorari to the Supreme Court was denied. He remained incarcerated for more than six years, still failing to repatriate the assets. The judge later apparently found that the incarceration had become punitive and released Lawrence.

Protect your assets **now**, *before* any claims arise.

Things to remember:

- The purpose of asset protection is to put your assets beyond the reach of creditors, or make it so expensive, difficult, and frustrating for creditors to come after your assets that they will either give up or be much more likely to settle reasonably.

- The emphasis of AP planning is to separate you from the ownership of your property while at the same time allowing you to keep the control and advantageous use of it.

- The most important thing to remember is to protect your assets BEFORE any claims arise.

CHAPTER 2

Offshore Planning

"The art is not in making money, but in keeping it."
~Proverb

How do I get "offshore?"

The definition of "offshore" in this context is any jurisdiction that resides outside your home country, its territories or commonwealths. Ideally, an offshore jurisdiction should provide you with some unique financial advantage.

Why would I want to go offshore?

There are myriad reasons to place your assets offshore. You might:

- be worried about market instability

- want to invest in foreign markets

- wish to protect your assets against lawsuits, frivolous and otherwise

- seek more privacy in your financial life

- need an estate plan for your family
- question the adequacy of your retirement plan
- desire simply to increase your wealth

What is an Offshore Asset Protection Trust and what can it do for me?

An Offshore Asset Protection Trust (OAPT) is a trust set up under the laws of a foreign jurisdiction in a way that is favorable to your circumstances. OAPTs are set up in essentially the same way as any other type of trust. However, because these trusts are designed primarily for asset protection, they are often self-settled, i.e., the grantor is designated as one of the beneficiaries.

While not exclusive to offshore trusts, OAPTs typically use trust **Protectors** appointed by the grantor to oversee the trustee to ensure he is doing his job. The Protector can overrule the trustee's decisions and even remove the existing trustee and appoint a new one, if necessary. For example, if local law requires the trustee to take actions that are not in the best interests of the trust, the Protector can appoint a new trustee in a different country, where such actions are not mandatory. Having this Protector adds an extra layer of protection to the trust. It also gives the grantor a little more control because the Protector is there to ensure that the grantor's wishes are being followed. The trust instrument can also contain a provision for the replacement of the Protector, if necessary.

Most offshore trusts also contain **flee** and **anti-duress** clauses. The flee clause empowers the trustee to move the trust, thereby changing the laws that govern it, in the face of an anticipated attack on the trust. The anti-duress clause allows the trustee to ignore a request for distributions from the trust, even if it is legal, if said request is made under duress. An example of this would be if a U.S. court ordered funds repatriated.

Another very important aspect of an OAPT is the freedom it gives you to invest. In the U.S., certain types of investments are prohibited. However, an offshore trust can invest as the trustee or the trust advisor sees fit (see directed trusts, Chapter 4).

When you set up your trust, you will be asked to prove that the source of your funds is legitimate. Be aware that banks and trust companies no longer accept cash, as the funds are not traceable.

Here are some of the many things Offshore Asset Protection Trusts can do:

- Run a professional or commercial business
- Own and invest in real estate, currencies, stocks, bonds, negotiable instruments and personal property
- Pay medical, educational and other expenses
- Provide for retirement
- Potentially lower inheritance taxes and avoid probate

What do I put in my OAPT?

You can put almost anything into an OAPT: bank accounts, brokerage accounts, luxury automobiles, yachts, even gold and other commodities. You can also place shares of domestic or offshore corporations in your trust. However you cannot place U.S. "S" Corporation stocks in your offshore trust as only U.S. **persons** may own stock in an "S" Corporation.

One of the things you should consider placing in your OAPT is a bank account.

What are the benefits of an offshore bank account?

The primary benefits of having an offshore bank account are:

- Investment opportunity and diversification
- Asset protection

It is important to ensure that your offshore bank does not maintain a branch office within the U.S. and that you restrict the use of your offshore account exclusively to offshore activities. In other words, you would not pay your U.S.-based utility bill with checks drawn on your offshore account. Offshore transactions must remain separate and independent. If you use your offshore account for a U.S.-related transaction, your offshore account may then fall under the jurisdiction of a U.S. court, thereby nullifying any benefit of maintaining an account offshore.

Be prepared to designate a beneficiary or grant another person co-ownership with rights of survivorship.

It is also important to ascertain the reputation and financial state of each offshore bank you are considering as well as evaluate the fee schedules. All documentation should be available in English, and all persons with whom you will be dealing should be fluent in English.

When you open your account, be prepared to identify yourself. You may be asked to provide your birth certificate, a valid passport, and/or a utility bill from home. You will be asked to show proof of the source of your funds. Again, because cash is virtually impossible to trace, it is unlikely that a reputable bank will accept it as a form of deposit.

Furthermore, any and all transfers made into your account will be monitored by the U.S. Government. Transfers of assets of $10,000 or more require the filing of appropriate forms with the IRS or the U.S. Customs and Border

Protection Agency. Almost always, the transferring bank will automatically file these forms on your behalf. An attempt to transfer $10,000 or more, broken up into lesser amounts in order to circumvent such reporting requirements (a process referred to as "structuring"), is considered to be a crime. This reporting requirement also applies to cash equivalents such as traveler's checks, bearer bonds, and negotiable instruments, which may be subject to immediate seizure.

The types of accounts you can have in an offshore bank account include:

- **current accounts** (checking, debit and credit)

- **deposit accounts** (savings over longer terms)

- **twin accounts** (a combination of current and deposit accounts)

- **fiduciary accounts** (an anonymous investment with the bank named as proxy investor)

- **certificates of deposit/CDs**

- **precious metals accounts** (investments in metals which the bank safeguards)

- **investment accounts** (bank-managed investments)

- **managed accounts** (similar to investment accounts but managed by account holder)

- **safekeeping accounts** (bank-managed deposit stocks, bonds and other valuables)

The days of the secret, numbered accounts are over.

What effect does Title V, Subtitle A, Part I §501(a) of the new HIRE Act, enacted March 18, 2010, have on offshore accounts?

The Hiring Incentives to Restore Employment Act (HIRE) was designed to create jobs by providing tax incentives, such as business credits, to those companies who hire new employees. However, raising the necessary revenue to offset such costs meant making significant changes in the rules governing foreign trusts, including broadening the current trust reporting requirements and penalties. A US owner of any percentage of a foreign trust under grantor trust provisions is obligated not only to provide information as required with respect to the foreign trust *but also ensure that the trustee complies with all reporting requirements.*

Essentially, the HIRE Act adds a new fourth chapter, §§1471–1474, to the Internal Revenue Code that specifically deals with offshore financial institutions and their U.S. customers. §1471(a) provides for a 30% tax on withholdable payments to said institutions if certain reporting requirements have not been met. These requirements are set forth in §1471(c) (1)(A-D). Essentially, for each U.S. account maintained, all foreign financial institutions must provide: (A) the name, address and tax identification number (TIN) of each U.S. account holder; or, if the account holder is a U.S. owned foreign entity, the name, address and TIN of each substantial U.S. owner of said entity; (B) the account number; (C) the account balance or value; and (D) gross receipts and gross withdrawals or payments from the account.

Under §1471(c)(2), the foreign financial institution can elect to report as if it were a U.S. financial institution pursuant to §§6041, 6042, 6045, and 6049 of the Internal Revenue Code. In that case, (C) and (D) would not apply; however, §6041 requires essentially the same information.

Pursuant to §1471(b)(1)(A-F), foreign financial institutions are required to enter into agreements with the U.S. to satisfy reporting requirements. These agreements provide that (A) the institution will collect whatever information necessary to determine if any account is a U.S account; (B) it will comply with verification and due diligence requirements to identify U.S. accounts; (C) it will report annually the required information with respect to all U.S. accounts; (D) that it will withhold a tax of 30% i) on any "passthru payments" to "recalcitrant account holders" or another non-compliant foreign financial institution, and ii) on any passthru payments to foreign financial institutions under other specified situations; and (F) **if, because of the prevailing laws, a waiver is necessary to provide the information required by this Act, the foreign financial institution will attempt to obtain a waiver for each U.S. account; if unable to do so, it will close that particular account.**

This is clearly meant to obviate the bank secrecy laws currently in place in several offshore jurisdictions. By requiring the account holder to sign a waiver or have the account closed, the U.S. Government is making it very difficult, if not impossible, for U.S. persons to enjoy banking privacy offshore.

A **financial account** for purposes of this Act is any depository or custodial account maintained by any financial institution, and any equity or debt interest in such a financial institution (excepting interests regularly traded on an established securities market). A **passthru payment** is essentially a **withholdable payment,** any type of payment with sources **inside** the U.S. A **recalcitrant account holder** is one who fails to provide either the required information or a waiver allowing the financial institution to do so.

A **United States Account** for the purposes of this Act is a financial account held by one or more U.S. persons or by a U.S.-owned foreign entity. But, if you are a natural person and your aggregate depository accounts in a financial institution do not exceed $50,000, you are not considered to possess a **United States Account** for the purposes of this Act.

A **foreign financial institution** is defined as any financial institution that is not a U.S. person or organized under the laws of a U.S. possession.

A **financial institution** is defined as any entity that accepts deposits in the ordinary course of a banking or similar business as a substantial portion of its business, holds financial assets for others or is primarily engaged (represented as such) in the business of investing, reinvesting, or trading its securities, partnership interests, commodities or any interest therein.

Lastly, a **United States foreign entity** is defined as any foreign entity that possesses one or more substantial U.S. owners.

How does this affect banking secrecy? It virtually eliminates it in any country wishing to do business with the U.S. The days of the banking haven are likely over for U.S. persons.

How do I choose where to go?

- *Common Law Jurisdictions:* These are jurisdictions that inherited English law. There are almost 60 current and former colonies to fall into this category. A valid trust can be formed in any one of them. But, because they have similar laws, they may honor each other's judgments.

  One of the holdovers from English law is a statute enacted in 1571 called the **Statute of Elizabeth**. This is from where our fraudulent conveyance rules originally derived. The Statute of Elizabeth, although long ago repealed in England, has held on in some form in many of the common law jurisdictions. The biggest problem it poses is that it allows transfers to be voided with respect to **future unknown** creditors. Therefore, it is best to choose a jurisdiction that has dealt with this statute by either repeal or modification. The Cook Islands, for example, have repealed it. Others have modified it so that it no longer applies to future unknown creditors.

- *Civil Law Jurisdictions:*

  Several civil law jurisdictions, countries whose laws are codified and where the principal basis of law is statutory, also have laws permitting trusts. These jurisdictions include Liechtenstein, Panama, Luxembourg, and Switzerland.

When deciding upon an offshore jurisdiction, verify that the chosen jurisdiction:

- Does not honor foreign judgments against validly formed trusts

- is politically and economically stable

- has acceptable rules regarding fraudulent conveyances

- has dealt with the **Statute of Elizabeth**. Another way your jurisdiction may circumvent the Statute of Elizabeth is to enact statutes of limitations which curtail the time a creditor has to bring his claim after the asset has been transferred.

- allows self-settled trusts.

- allows dynasty trusts and has favorably modified the rule against perpetuities.

- does not tax the trust's offshore income of non-residents. Most do not; or, if they do, it is limited solely to any portion deemed to be domestic income.

- permits use of the "flee clause" to quickly change jurisdictions and thus the law controlling the trust.

Many offshore jurisdictions do not honor foreign money judgments, which puts the creditor in the unenviable position of having to re-litigate his case on foreign soil, and likely with foreign lawyers. To reiterate a point made in the preceding chapter, one purpose of these trusts is to either place your assets beyond the reach of creditors or to make it so prohibitively expensive, difficult and frustrating for creditors to come after your assets as to assure reasonable settlement or abandonment.

In addition to not recognizing U.S. judgments, many jurisdictions have brief statutes of limitations for fraudulent transfers. This means that a creditor has less time to bring his claim than he would in the U.S. In the U.S., the statute is typically four years, though it varies by state. The statute in the Cook Islands is one year, while in the Bahamas and Gibraltar it is two years or less. In Gibraltar, there is no statutory period for transfers made while the settlor is solvent. This law provides for immediate protection for those assets of the trust. The burden is on the creditor to show that the transfer rendered the settlor insolvent. These shorter statutes of limitations mean that the creditor must discover his claim within the statutory period, or he is forever barred from bringing it. And, if you are a creditor trying to attack a trust in the Cook Islands, you have to prove **beyond a reasonable doubt** that the settlor intended to defraud you. That is no easy standard; criminal cases are decided using this standard of proof.

Even in those jurisdictions that may not have the strongest asset protection laws, the mere fact that the assets are out of the U.S. and that creditors must bring legal action in a foreign court gives the jurisdiction asset protection advantages.

What is a tax haven?

Tax havens offer low or no taxes, financial security, solid currencies, secrecy and they are completely legal. Panama and Switzerland are prime examples of tax havens, welcoming foreigners without imposing taxes on their financial dealings. As of 2008, more than $50 trillion dollars in personal wealth — almost half of the entire world's personal wealth — resided in approximately 60 tax and asset havens throughout the world, including Hong Kong and Panama. However, one-third of that wealth was stashed in Switzerland's bank vaults.

In addition to the above, tax havens also offer:

- greater choice in potentially more profitable investment opportunities

- smart, efficient estate planning

- healthy asset protection

- less burdensome business regulations

- the potential to establish dual citizenship and, with it, obtain a second passport (not all tax havens afford this)

How do I secure an appropriate trustee?

The safest way to secure an appropriate trustee is through your professional asset protection advisor. The OFC Report, an annual publication, contains articles on various offshore jurisdictions, and provides a list of trustees and other professionals within those jurisdictions along with their contact information. Make sure your potential trustee is willing to sign all of the required IRS forms annually, including but not limited to Form 3520 (Annual Return to Report Transactions with Foreign Trusts and Receipt of Certain Foreign Gifts) and Form 3520A (Annual Information Return of Foreign Trust with a US Owner). Trustees must be aware of their US tax reporting obligations in order to ensure that you, the creator of the trust, are not penalized. Penalties will be imposed upon you if they refuse. It is important to note that offshore trusts are not tax avoidance devices since US tax residents and citizens are required to report their worldwide income.

Sometimes it is more important to find the right trustee than to locate the perfect trust jurisdiction. You will be giving legal title to your assets to this person and trusting him or her to follow your directives, possibly for years to come. You need a trustee who is not a U.S. citizen, and does not conduct any business in the U.S. that could enable the trustee to fall under U.S. jurisdiction.

Things to remember:

- Thoroughly research your potential trust jurisdictions to determine which has the best features for you, such as favorable fraudulent conveyance rules or political and economic stability.
    - offshore asset protection trusts can add extra layers of protection to your asset protection plan:
    - flee and anti-duress clauses may be added for added security;
- Creditors often have shorter statutes of limitation to challenge your transfers into the trust.
- Offshore bank accounts can handle all sorts of transactions, from checking to investing in precious metals.
    - Be prepared to identify yourself and the source of your funds.
    - Banking secrecy may be null and void with respect to U.S. persons due to the new HIRE Act.

CHAPTER 3

Does Situs Matter?

A place for everything, everything in its place. ~Benjamin Franklin

Let me answer this with a resounding YES! Situs does matter!

Which are the best states for asset protection?

More and more states are beginning to compete for trust business. As a result, there are many varying state laws out there from which to choose. If your focus is on making the most money you can with your trust, you should zero in on those states that do not levy an income tax on trusts. If you are interested in leaving your estate for future generations, there are states that allow so-called dynasty trusts, which last anywhere from 150 years to forever. However, if you are most concerned with legal liability, a state that allows DAPTs (domestic asset protection trusts) might work best for you. These trusts are set up to protect assets from claimants.

As discussed in Chapter 1, Alaska was the first state to enact anti-creditor trust legislation. South Dakota, Delaware, and Nevada are some of the best of the remaining jurisdictions that have such legislation, with short statutes of limitations.

South Dakota has the best privacy statute in the US. a total seal, as opposed to Delaware, where trusts are only sealed for three years. In Alaska and the remaining states, trust documents are typically open to public review. South Dakota and Alaska levy no state income taxes on trusts. Further, in South Dakota, there are no capital gains, dividend, interest, or intangible taxes on trusts. Delaware, on the other hand, does tax its residents.

In 1979, the Murphy case was decided, wherein the IRS conceded that trusts could have unlimited durations. South Dakota and a few other states have followed this case and now have unlimited trust durations, abrogating (abolishing) the rule against perpetuities in those states. This and similarly situated trusts are called dynasty trusts (see below). Unlike South Dakota, Alaska and Delaware each has a thousand-year limit on trusts and attaches other circumstances. However, Delaware also limits real estate to 110 years, unless the real estate is placed in an LLC or partnership. But, the potential dangers in that setup are clear: if the LLC or partnership is dissolved, the real estate is limited again, and the entire trust may be tainted. Nevada only has a 365-year statute.

- *Dynasty Trusts:* These are trusts that exist under the laws of several states and foreign jurisdictions that have either abolished or altered the rule against perpetuities. Before this, trusts could not endure for more than 21 years beyond the death of the last beneficiary who was alive at the time of the trust's creation.

  Generally, every time someone's assets pass from one generation to another, gift and estate taxes are levied. Dynasty trusts effectively create successive estates, thereby avoiding these taxes. These estates can outlive immediate family members and continue to provide for future generations. Of course, this benefit only adheres so long as the assets remain in trust. Otherwise, the trust is subject to the Generation Skipping Tax (GST), a flat tax to those two or more generations below the grantor, in addition to estate taxes, which will have their maximum at 55% in 2011. However, you can still maintain a limited exemption from the GST. While it is unfortunate that the exemption plummets from $3.5 million in 2009 to $1 million in 2011, those with moderate estates can still benefit.

You can set a dynasty trust up wherever you live, as long as the trustee is in the jurisdiction where you want your trust to be. Several states that allow dynasty trusts have strong asset protection laws as well, making them favorable jurisdictions for your trust. Also, you'll want to choose a state that does not impose income tax on trust assets.

Delaware is arguably the only place in the world that extends you complete privacy when it comes to your LLC or limited partnership (LP). You can set up there, furnishing nothing more than the name of your attorney. You don't even have to name your managing member! Delaware is also one of the few states that allow **Series LLCs** (see below).

However, South Dakota is one of the foremost states for asset protection statutes involving LLCs and family limited partnerships (FLPs). While the level of protection varies by state, the best protection is where the sole remedy available to the creditor is a charging order. South Dakota is such a state (SDCL §48-7-703). A charging order allows the creditor to collect the member's distributions, if and when they are distributed (see below). At best, this becomes a waiting game, with the creditor either going away, or settling for something nominal.

In addition, South Dakota is the first state to define a beneficiary's rights in trust. The South Dakota statute provides that neither a discretionary interest in a trust, nor limited powers of appointment, nor remainder interests are, in fact, property interests. This can be crucial in asset protection. Furthermore, the statute provides that neither a beneficiary nor a creditor can force a trustee to make a discretionary distribution.

If you have set up an OAPT or an APT in another state and wish to move the assets home or just elsewhere, what do you do? In South Dakota and Delaware, you can move your assets pursuant to state "tacking" provisions (SDCL 55-16-11 and Del. Code tit. 12, sec. 3332(2010)). But, you must be careful. These statutes will allow you to repatriate your assets or move them from one state to another and maintain your original disposition (transfer) date for fraudulent conveyance purposes, however, you must meet your state's criteria for the transfer. In South Dakota, the original disposition must be irrevocable pursuant to SDCL 55-16-2(2) and the original trust document must limit the original transferor's (or beneficiary's) ability to dispose of his interest in said trust (SDCL 55-16-2(3)). Remember, before you move anything, make sure you meet all relevant statutory definitions.

Another unique feature of South Dakota trust law is the Decanting, Reformation and Modification Statute. This can be used to modernize the administration of an existing trust. This component is very inexpensive and time efficient. Furthermore, it does not require judicial oversight.

Decanting statutes allow a trustee with discretionary distribution authority to modify the terms of a trust by transferring all of its assets to a new trust. In this way, the trustee can, for instance, make it a directed trust.

More on South Dakota trust statutes

The South Dakota Self-Settled Trust Statute, or State Bill (SB) 93, as it was originally introduced, became effective as of July 1, 2005. This South Dakota Statute, which was modeled on the Delaware Qualified Dispositions in Trust Act of 1997, authorizes "qualified dispositions" in a trust. As a result, assets are protected from the claims of certain creditors. A qualified disposition occurs when the settlor (grantor) transfers assets to a trustee or trustees, with or without consideration.

Certain requirements must be fulfilled in order to meet the necessary criteria for obtaining this authorization. First, a written trust instrument that expressly incorporates South Dakota trust law must be created. Second, the trust must be irrevocable and contain a spendthrift provision. A spendthrift clause, as mentioned before, is one of the major facets of this type of trust and is included to prevent a beneficiary from alienating his or her expected interests in favor of a creditor.

The trustee named to oversee this trust must be an individual resident of South Dakota. Alternatively, the trustee may be an institutional trustee, which is authorized to act in South Dakota and is therefore subject to the supervision of the South Dakota Division of Banking, the Federal Deposit Insurance Corporation (FDIC), the Office of the Comptroller of the Currency (OCC), or the Office of Thrift Supervision (OTS).

According to the provisions of the South Dakota Self-Settled Trust Statute, custody of the trust's assets and the material administration of those assets must occur within the state of South Dakota.

The settlor retains the right to veto proposed distributions from the trust assets. Also, the settlor is permitted to appoint or remove a trustee or trust advisor (SDCL §55-16-2).

A trust protector may also be appointed. In fact, in 1997, South Dakota became the first state to introduce statutory law concerning the appointment of a trust protector (SDCL §55-16-4). As you recall, a trust protector essentially oversees the trustee and adds an extra layer of protection and control to your AP trust.

South Dakota trusts, like other DAPTs, are self-settled spendthrift trusts. This means that a settlor creates a trust for his own benefit, naming himself as a beneficiary, in order to protect funds in the event that creditors make a legal claim against the settlor's personal or business assets. Any qualified dispositions to the trust will be protected from attachment or other legal claims so long as they do not fall within any statutory exceptions.

Certain transfers are not considered qualified dispositions for purposes of the South Dakota Statute. First, if a creditor's claim arose on or before the date of the qualified disposition and the creditor brings action within three years of the disposition, the transaction may be considered a fraudulent transfer pursuant to SDCL §55-16-10. He may also bring an action within three years if his claim arose **after** the qualified disposition. But, in all cases, the creditor must show the transfers were made with the intent to defraud by furnishing **clear and convincing evidence** (SDCL §§55-16-9 and 55-16-10(2)).

Other exceptions include any domestic relations obligations or the legal settlement of claims that arose before the qualified disposition was made. Likewise, a personal injury claim filed on or before the date of the qualified disposition serves as an exception to these rules (SDCL §55-16-15(1) and (2)).

Trustees, trust advisors and trust preparers are immune from prosecution in connection with these exceptions provided that they acted within their legal boundaries in fulfilling their duties to the trust (SDCL §55-16-12).

Who benefits from a South Dakota trust?

South Dakota trusts are extremely attractive options for professionals who practice in high-risk specialty areas. In fact, they're ideal for anyone with assets to protect. When this trust is used in conjunction with dynasty capability, perpetual protection is available to the trust's assets. A South Dakota trust also provides the comfort and convenience of local liaisons with whom it is easier to interact than offshore trustees. A trust such as this can even be a cost-effective alternative to maintaining expensive liability insurance in the event of a negligence or malpractice claim, **if properly structured**.

A South Dakota DAPT offers a legal, United States-based way to protect your hard-earned assets and wealth. These trusts are also designed to provide bankruptcy asset protection. Such wealth protection strategies are popular among doctors, lawyers, celebrities, executives, and other moderately high and high income individuals. Capricious judges, misinformed, envious juries, and unexpected financial reversals can ravage your life savings. A domestic Asset Protection Trust, if correctly established in advance by a competent attorney, can provide legal protection for your home, cars, boats and other liquid and non-liquid assets of any dollar value. Please note, however, that the testing of these trusts (including bankruptcy asset protection cases), in U.S. courts to date is limited, so judges have little precedent to guide them.

More on Alaska trust statutes

The Alaska Trust Act provides for protection from creditor attack when the specified transfers are made into a trust whose trust instrument contains a spendthrift clause. It is not necessary that the trust be self-settled, but the protections of the Act will apply if it is. Such a trust is protected from creditor attack, unless the creditor is a creditor of the settlor *and* the creditor shows by **clear and convincing evidence** that the settlor's transfer of assets was with the **intent** to defraud that creditor *and* the creditor's actions comply with the extinguishment rules of Alaska Stat. 34.40.110(d). That statute allows for claims to be brought before the latter of either four years from the date of transfer, or one year from when a claim was or should reasonably have been discovered by the creditor (if the creditor can meet other specified requirements). Significantly, Alaska has put in its statute that a settlor's **expressed** intention to protect beneficiaries from potential future creditors is **not** evidence of intent to defraud (Alaska Stat. Sec. 34.40.110(b)(1)).

The Alaska Trust Act excludes revocable trusts from protection against creditors, an issue mentioned in Chapters 1 and 3. With certain exceptions, you also will not be protected if all or part of the trust's principal, income or both are to be distributed to the settlor. Finally, if the transfer is made when the settlor is 30 or more days in default on child support, the protections of Alaska Stat. Sec. 34.40.110(b) will not apply.

Even if you should lose against a creditor, your entire trust is not at risk. Only the particular transfer at issue is subject to the creditor's reach. Furthermore, only the trust assets and the settlor are subject to attack. The trustee and all related parties are immune, pursuant to Alaska Stat. Sec. 34.40.110(e). Alaska claims exclusive jurisdiction over all causes of action arising under Alaska Stat. Sec. 34.40.110.(b)(1).

The protections of this Act still apply even if the settlor, who may be the sole beneficiary, is also a co-trustee or trust advisor, as long as he doesn't have power over discretionary distributions. If the beneficiary is not the settlor, the protections apply whether that beneficiary acts as sole trustee, co-trustee or trust advisor.

The settlor has the following additional powers, which do not affect the protections provided by the Act:

- To appoint a trustee, a trust protector or a trust advisor

- To remove and appoint replacement trustees and trust protectors, provided that the replacements comply with 26 U.S.C. 672(c)

- To remove and appoint a replacement advisor

When naming yourself as a beneficiary under the Act, you must sign a sworn affidavit that states the following:

- You have full right, title and authority to transfer assets to the trust

- The transfer will not render you insolvent

- You do not intend to defraud a creditor by transferring your assets to the trust

- You have no pending or threatened court actions against you, except those which you have set forth on an attachment to the affidavit

- You have no pending or threatened administrative proceedings against you, except those which you have set forth on an attachment to the affidavit

- You are not currently in default of a child support obligation by more than 30 days

- You are not contemplating filing bankruptcy

- The assets you are transferring were not derived through unlawful activities

A beneficiary's interest in a trust is not considered property for purposes of marital property division in the event of divorce. Not so with the settlor of a self-settled trust (Alaska Stat. Sec. 34.40.110(l)). Unless otherwise agreed to in writing, the section does not apply to assets transferred after the marriage or within 30 days of it, and those assets are available for distribution unless the settlor gives written notice to his spouse or intended spouse of the transfer.

Alaska Stat. Sec. 13.36.370 provides for the appointment of a trust protector in the trust instrument whose powers can include:

- Removing and appointing a trustee

- Modifying or amending the trust instrument to improve tax status or keep up with changes in laws, regulations, etc.

- Increasing or decreasing the interests of any beneficiary to the trust

- Modifying the terms of a power of appointment granted by the trust.

The trust protector is not liable or accountable as a trustee or fiduciary as a result of any act or omission of the trust protector when acting under powers granted by the trust instrument.

Likewise, any trust advisor appointed is so immune. The trust advisor can advise the trustee on all matters involving the trust, but the trustee is under no obligation to follow said advice (Alaska Stat. Sec. 13.36.375).

A powerful feature of Alaska law is contained in Alaska Stat. Sec. 13.36.043, which allows you to move your trust to Alaska from wherever it might be, whether another state or another country. As long as it was valid when created, Alaska will honor it. Even perpetual trusts are allowed. Provided that Alaska law does not prohibit the provisions of your trust, they will be enforceable. Alaska does not even require that you comply with their laws in the creation of your trust.

Finally, in order for Alaska law to govern your trust:

- Some or all of the trust assets must be deposited in Alaska and be administered by a qualified person.

"Deposited" means a checking account, time deposit, certificate of deposit, brokerage account, trust company fiduciary account, or other similar account or deposit located in Alaska. "Qualified person" means (1) an individual whose permanent residence is in Alaska, or (2) a trust company organized under Alaska Stat. Sec. 6.26 with its principal place of business in Alaska, or (3) a bank organized under Alaska Stat. Sec. 06.05, or a national banking association organized under 12 U.S.C. 21 - 216d, if said bank or national banking association had and exercised trust powers and had its principal place of business in Alaska (Alaska Stat. Sec. 13.36.390).

- At least one trustee is a qualified person designated by the trust instrument or by a court having jurisdiction over the trust

- The powers of this trustee include or are limited to:

  - Maintaining trust records

  - Seeing that the income tax for the trust is filed

- Part or all of the administration of the trust must occur in Alaska, including the physical maintenance of records for the trust (Alaska Stat. Sec. 13.36.035(c)).

More on Delaware trust statutes

Delaware's Qualified Dispositions in Trust Act has been the model for many states' asset protection statutes. Under this Act, a qualified disposition in trust is proof against all actions unless they are brought pursuant to the fraudulent conveyance provisions of Del. Code Tit. 6 §§ 1304 and 1305. A creditor who seeks to bring a claim that arose after a qualified disposition was made must show that the qualified disposition was made with the **actual intent** to defraud. Del. Code Tit. 6 §1304 delineates the requirements for finding a transaction fraudulent with respect to a present or future creditor. Here, the creditor must show that a transfer was made or an obligation incurred with the **actual intent** to hinder, delay or defraud any creditor. This section includes eleven badges of fraud for use in determining actual intent. Del. Code Tit. 6 §1305 deals with fraudulent transfers as to present creditors alone. While Del. Code Tit. 6 §1304 dealt with the subjective test for actual fraud that we have discussed before, this section applies a more objective test, as for constructive fraud. As you recall, that was, and is the standard here.

- Did the transferor receive fair market value; and

- Was the transferor insolvent at the time, or did he become so as a result of the transaction?

Delaware adds an additional standard to the mix. It is also considered to be a fraudulent transfer in Delaware if the transferor transfers the asset to an "insider" for a prior debt, when the transferor was insolvent, *and* the insider had reason to believe the transferor was insolvent.

In all such actions, the burden is on the creditor to prove his case by furnishing **clear and convincing evidence**. This is a heightened standard of proof from most civil matters, although it is less than a criminal standard.

Recovery is limited to the disposition in question and only to the extent necessary to satisfy the debt to the creditor, together with costs. Furthermore, if there has been no showing of bad faith on the part of the trustee, he gets to satisfy his defense costs out of the disposition first! (Del. Code Tit. 12 § 3574(a) and (b).)

A creditor's claim is extinguished if he does not bring it within four years of the qualified disposition, if his claim arose at the same time or after the disposition. If it arose before the disposition he can bring it within four years from the disposition or, if later, one year from the date he did or reasonably should have discovered his claim (Del. Cod Tit. 12 §3572(b) and Del. Code Tit. 6 § 1309(3)).

Pursuant to Del. Code Tit. 12 §3572(d) and (e), a trustee, advisor and any person involved with the counseling, drafting, preparation, execution or funding of a trust that is the subject of a qualified distribution is immune from creditor attack.

A **Qualified Disposition** is essentially a transfer, conveyance or assignment of property from one or more transferors to one or more trustees, one of whom must be a qualified trustee with or without consideration, through the use of a trust instrument. A **Qualified Trustee** is a natural person who is a resident of Delaware or, if not a natural person, is authorized by the laws of Delaware to act as a trustee and is subject to supervision by the Bank Commissioner of the State, the FDIC, the Comptroller of the Currency, or the Office of Thrift Supervision, or any of their successors; and materially participates in the administration of the trust, including, keeping or arranging for the custody of some or all of the trust assets in Delaware, maintaining trust records, and ensuring that the fiduciary income tax returns for the trust are prepared (Del. Code Tit. 12 § 3570 (8) a. and b.).

The protections of this Act do not accrue to 1) orders for child or spousal support or to marital divisions of property (but only to the extent of the debt owed) or 2) to any person who suffers death, personal injury or property damage on or before the qualified disposition, which was caused in whole or in part by the tortious act or omission of the transferor or one for whom he was vicariously liable (but only to the extent of the claim) (Del. Code Tit. 12 § 3573).

Delaware does **not** allow the transferor to be a trustee, but the transferor may serve as an investment advisor. Delaware provides for the appointment of several advisors, which term includes trust protector, as that term is understood. The following advisors are specifically authorized:

- Those with authority to remove and appoint qualified trustees and trust advisors

- Those with authority to direct, consent to or disapprove distributions from the trust

- Investment advisers and trust protectors, even if they do not meet the requirements of a qualified trustee (Del. Code Tit. 12 §§ 3570(8)c.3 and 3313)

To be subject to the protections delineated above, a Delaware trust must expressly incorporate the laws of Delaware into the trust instrument and be irrevocable. You will need a spendthrift clause as well. The settlor retains a number of powers that do not render the trust instrument revocable. Some of these are:

- To veto a distribution

- A limited power of appointment

- The right to receive income

- The right to remove a trustee or advisor and to appoint a new trustee or advisor

- The right to use real property held under a qualified personal residence trust

- The right to have the qualified trustee pay his last expenses

Remember, all of these powers must be clearly set forth in the trust instrument to be effective (Del. Code Tit. 12 §3570(11)b).

What are the main weaknesses of the DAPT?

The first weakness I would note is that, unless you live in a state that has a strong asset protection statute, it may not be worth taking the chance that, for example, a Florida judge will honor South Dakota trust law. In fact, South Dakota itself states that a trustee as well as the trust property has to be in South Dakota for its laws to apply. Importing the laws of other states to enjoy favorable trust statutes in your own state has yet to be tested.

Next, the trustee is subject to U.S. jurisdiction — no ignoring orders and no fleeing.

Third, full faith and credit applies. Whereas, in some offshore jurisdictions, the creditor may have to start his case all over again.

Which offshore jurisdictions are best?

Again, this depends on your ultimate goal.

There are at least five factors you should consider when deciding which jurisdiction is ultimately the best for you:

- The political stability of the government
- Whether its laws are favorable for foreign investors
- Whether the laws provide a wide enough variety of legal entities for your asset protection and estate planning needs
- Whether it has bank secrecy laws and appropriate financial privacy (see the new HIRE act, Chapter 2)
- Whether it will impose taxes on you

If you are looking for some place to bank, obtain U.S. tax-deferred annuities, life insurance, or enjoy asset protection, Liechtenstein, nestled between Switzerland and Austria, is the place for you. However, like so many previous privacy and tax havens, Liechtenstein has entered into a tax treaty with the U.S. and agreed to honor Article 29 of the Organization for Economic and Community Development, a model tax information exchange treaty. Now, Liechtenstein, Switzerland and others will provide information on foreign tax evasion when their governments order them to do so.

Notwithstanding this development, another plus to Liechtenstein is that creditors who have to bring their action there are quite discouraged when they also discover that they must handle all matters in the German language!

Some additional reputable banking havens are Switzerland, Panama, Nevis, Belize, Austria, Denmark, Singapore, Hong Kong, Jersey, the Cayman Islands and Gibraltar. Be prepared to pay some large minimum balances for the privilege of banking in these locations however. Private banks hover around $25,000 for their opening balances and for Switzerland and Liechtenstein you are looking at about $100,000 to open an account, unless you want to open it at one of the large Swiss banks like UBS or Julius Baer, in which case be prepared to put up a cool million.

If you are looking for a jurisdiction with strong OAPT laws, look at the Cook Islands — a favorite jurisdiction — Belize, Nevis and The Bahamas. Be advised, however, that the courts of at least two of these jurisdictions, the Cook Islands and The Bahamas, have nullified their own trust laws when trusts were used fraudulently. Some consider these jurisdictions to have extreme laws. More moderate OAPT laws can be found in Bermuda and the Cayman Islands.

The following are examples of jurisdictions that have no AP specifications in their trust laws: the Isle of Man, Jersey, Guernsey, and the British Virgin Islands, but just the fact that they are offshore may give them some asset protection advantages. And don't overlook their other haven attributes. For instance, the Isle of Man levies no taxes on corporations and is recommended if you are looking to invest in life insurance or annuities.

Another consideration is whether or not to avoid jurisdictions that are not sovereign nations. Currently, U.K. territories such as the British Virgin Islands and the Cayman Islands remain answerable to the parliament of the U.K. That means they can be made to levy withholding taxes on interest earned and disclose the identity of all parties of a private trust.

Some jurisdictions, such as the Cook Islands, St. Vincent and Samoa, don't have many banks or lawyers or trustees from which to choose. This could make it difficult to change trustees or if you need to litigate.

If secrecy and confidentiality are your goal, choose one of the English law jurisdictions. They hold a duty of confidentiality between bankers and their customers. In fact, bank secrecy laws that punish the violator of said duty with fines or prison time have been enacted in The Bahamas, the Cook Islands, the Cayman Islands, and the Turks & Caicos Islands. (Note: the new HIRE act was designed to counteract this. These banks may now be required to obtain waivers of these laws from their U.S. customers if they want to do any business with the U.S.)

Some additional trust-friendly nations are Panama, Singapore, and Liechtenstein.

Things to Remember

- DAPTs can be a good alternative to offshore AP methods when properly structured and *sitused*.

- South Dakota has the foremost DAPT and LLC laws in the U.S. If your situs is South Dakota, you can reap all of the benefits of these progressive statutes.

- Where you put your AP structure is as important as what structure you use.

- Choosing a foreign jurisdiction requires diligent research.

- Do you want the strongest AP laws?

- Is your jurisdiction sovereign?

- Will it impose taxes on you?

- Are there few banks, lawyers, or trustees?

- Is there bank secrecy? (See the discussion of the new HIRE Act, Chapter 2.)

- Can you form your AP structure there?

CHAPTER 4

Why a Directed Trust?

We can tell our values by looking at our checkbook stubs.
~Gloria Steinem

What is a directed trust?

Simply stated, a **directed trust** is where you turn over your assets to the trustee, but they are managed by someone else. A good example is a trust that is made up entirely of investments. The trustee has legal title to them, and the right to make distributions under the trust agreement, but another individual or firm is managing the investments. This type of arrangement must be allowed by either state statute or the trust laws of the country in which you are settling your trust.

In the U.S., South Dakota seems to have set the standard for such statutes due to the clear manner in which it delineates the responsibilities of the advisor and the trustee. Utah is very similar in this regard. South Dakota even permits settlors to appoint distribution advisors who can instruct the trustee to make a distribution, or withhold it. This is something like the trust protector arrangement we've already talked about in Chapters 2 and 3.

While a directed trust allows the grantor to choose who he wants to manage the assets of his trust in the trust document, a **delegated trust** is somewhat different. In a delegated trust, the trustee delegates the management duties to an advisor or other entity.

Currently, about 25 states in the U.S. and the District of Columbia have statutes that provide for delegated trusts, directed trusts, or some blending of the two. However, not all of them provide the same protection for the trustee with respect to the directing party. In Alabama, Arkansas, DC, Florida, Kansas, Maine, Missouri, Nebraska, New Hampshire, New Mexico, North Carolina, Oregon, Pennsylvania, South Carolina, Texas, Virginia and Wyoming, whose statutes follow §808(b) of the Uniform Trust Code, trustees are liable if what they are directed to do obviously conflicts with the trust's terms. They are also liable if they know that what they are being asked to do is a severe violation of the directing party's fiduciary duty. In addition to South Dakota, the following states have directed trust statutes that provide substantial protection for the trustee: Colorado, Delaware, Georgia, Idaho, Ohio, Oklahoma, Tennessee and Utah. In these states, his liability ranges from none at all to poor implementation of direction to willful misconduct.

In order to be deemed a directed trust, the trust contract must contain language that separates the investment from the administrative duties. All 50 states allow for judicial modification of these trust documents, but it isn't always easy. State requirements vary. In about 12 states, non-judicial settlement agreements (NJSAs) are permitted. These allow beneficiaries (and all interested parties) to sign a document agreeing to changes in the terms of the original trust. But, they do not allow changes to be made to the terms that govern distributions and other monetary matters.

How does a directed trust help fortify my assets?

With a directed trust, you alone determine who will invest and manage your assets, not your trustee. This gives you yet another layer of control. You can even insert more levels of control by adding one or more additional fiduciaries: a distribution advisor to watch over the trustee's handling of distributions and a trust protector to watch over the trustee in general.

Things to remember:

- In a directed trust, only you decide who will invest and manage your assets, while the trustee administers the trust.

- In a delegated trust, the trustee chooses who will manage your assets.

- With a directed trust and a few additional fiduciaries, such as a distributions advisor and a trust protector, you can add several layers of protection and control to your trust.

CHAPTER 5

Other Techniques to Consider

The real measure of your wealth is how much you'd be worth if you lost all your money. ~Author unknown

What is an LLC and how can I use it?

A limited liability company (LLC) is a legal entity that is made up of members who hold interests in it. It is governed by an operating agreement and set up by articles of organization. There are certain formalities that must be followed, though arguably less cumbersome than those of a corporation, in order to enjoy the substantial protections afforded by LLCs.

While no state requires an LLC to hold meetings or keep minutes, they are certainly required to pay taxes. If you ignore the form of the LLC by failing to do so, maybe failing to open a separate bank account as well, a creditor might be able to "pierce the corporate veil" of your LLC and get to your personal assets. However, if you treat the LLC as a separate entity, a creditor usually won't be able to reach a member's personal assets.

The LLC has pass-through taxation wherein its members are taxed at their individual rates on their individual shares. This effectively solves the double taxation issue we see with corporations.

One other difference between LLCs and corporations, such as IBCs (international business corporations), is that, with an LLC, if a member dies or goes bankrupt, the LLC is dissolved. The IBC or standard corporation can go on forever.

An LLC is a powerful asset protection tool for several reasons:

- It is ideal for insulating high-risk assets

- There are no physical shares for a creditor to attach

- A managing member cannot be forced to distribute assets, e.g., in the case of a charging order, when a creditor obtains a judgment against the assets of a member — see below

- It is ideal for insulating valuable property, like trademarks, patents, copyrights and other intellectual property. These can then be licensed back to the operating company. (That way, if the operating company should go bankrupt, you won't lose the trade name and /or trademark that you put in the LLC.)

- It is also ideal for holding real estate and equipment that can then be leased back to an operating company, insulating them from creditor collection since creditors cannot get at the assets of a properly formed and maintained LLC.

- You can make an LLC the beneficiary of your trust to avoid the self-settled trust problem.

If you have high-risk assets to protect, the LLC is a great way to go. Always use a separate legal structure for each high-risk asset, such as an apartment building or medical practice. LLCs are ideal for this with their membership structure, allowing each member to be insulated, as long as formalities are followed. The reason for separating your assets this way is, if you put them all in the same structure and a creditor does breach it, all of the assets in that structure can be reached.

- *Charging order protection.* When a creditor obtains a judgment against a member of an LLC, generally, the judge can only order the LLC to make that member's distributions to the creditor. The creditor obtains no management rights and no rights to any assets of the LLC. What he gets is something like a garnishment of wages. But, the creditor doesn't get the money until the LLC **chooses to** make the distribution; it can't be forced. Of course, this doesn't work if you have a small interest in a large LLC, where you wield little or no authority. You or a trusted friend must be the one in control of the LLC.

- *Foreclosure of member's interest.* Forty-one states still allow judicial foreclosure of a member's interest at a sheriff's sale. The member's interest is sold for a portion of what it is worth to satisfy the creditor's claim. Now, the purchaser owns the share, but he has no rights to management or to any specific partnership assets. He just has the rights to the distributions, arguably forever, and must pay taxes on this share. The former member may still owe a deficiency to the creditor and has lost his share in the LLC or LP.

  The nine states that do not allow foreclosures are Alabama, Alaska, Arizona, Delaware, Florida, North Dakota, South Dakota, Texas and Virginia.

- *Poison pill.* Written into the operating agreement, this clause allows the members of an LLC, for a nominal price, to buy out another member in the event of duress, a lawsuit, a charging order, or whatever conditions they set.

What are Series LLCs?

Series LLCs are essentially large LLCs with several different "cells." If you maintain separated books for each one, i.e., each "series," the liabilities of each are kept separate from one another. This way you could have your ten apartment houses in one LLC, each in its individual series. Nevada, Delaware and Illinois all allow series LLCs. The real question is whether other states will allow you to import the law of one of these other states into yours in order to create a series LLC.

What is a Family Limited Partnership?

An FLP is essentially a limited partnership held between family members, involving family assets. It is set up by filing the proper forms and filing fees for any LP. Often, the parents are the general partners, each holding a one or two percent share, while the children are designated as limited partners. Tax liability can be reduced by shifting income to the lower tax bracket limited partners (children over 14 years of age).

The FLP can hold business risks within other asset protection structures, such as trusts, but it should not itself engage in any business activities that could expose the family assets to risk. If the partnership itself does not get sued, then the primary (if not the sole) remedy for creditors is the charging order, which we have already discussed in this chapter.

Some planners believe that only business assets should be transferred into the FLP. Real estate should not be transferred into the FLP and you should **never** render yourself insolvent with your transfers. You should always have enough to live on without the assets in the FLP.

What is an International Business Corporation?

An IBC is a legal offshore tax-free entity, most often a limited liability company or corporation, that is set up in a foreign country that has enacted greater financial privacy laws than exist in the United States, which is not permitted to conduct any business in the foreign country in which it has been registered. IBCs are legal in various foreign locations, including Anguilla, Antigua, the British Virgin Islands, the Bahamas, Belize, Gibraltar, Nevis, Panama and Seychelles.

You retain 100 percent control over the IBC's assets without holding a managerial position and while maintaining maximum privacy and asset protection.

Typically, IBCs include:

- exemption from local corporate taxation, provided the IBC conducts no local business;

- no annual tax returning filing requirement;

- broad corporate authority to conduct varied businesses and activities;

- complete confidentiality of ownership;

- the ability to issue registered shares (bearer shares, once also common, have been subject recently to far greater restrictions if not outright elimination);

- exemption from having to appoint local officers or directors; and

- provision to appoint a local registered agent.

IBCs are most often used for offshore banking purposes to conduct investment activities (including stocks, bonds, mutual funds, certificates of deposit and term deposits) and international trade, including but not limited to buying and selling goods and services, operating businesses, holding bank accounts (including a corporate credit card used to cover legitimate related expenses) and real as well as intellectual property and e-business.

Annual fees assessed are nominal, usually a few hundred dollars, and limited to agent fees and company registration taxes. IBCs and their shareholders are exempt from offshore business license fees, corporate taxes, capital gains taxes, income taxes and any other income- or distribution-based taxes in connection with any of its transactions.

As no international tax identification number is required in order to open an IBC bank account, complete privacy is assured. IBC ownership records are not public and, in fact, it is illegal for a banker to reveal the identity of any owner or director of an IBC bank account to any individual outside the bank in which the account is held. However, it is important to ensure that an agent's contact information is always kept up to date.

IBCs have unlimited lifespans, making them a viable way of passing ownership to beneficiaries and legally bypassing inheritance, capital gains and income taxes.

It is recommended that you choose a country in which business is conducted in English and which is both independent and politically stable. Choosing a country within several hours of your own time zone is also an asset.

It is important to note, however, that all US citizens and tax residents are required to report their worldwide income and informational returns with the US Treasury Department and IRS each year and reveal all pertinent information relating to the IBC. Furthermore, it is very difficult for a US shareholder of an IBC to achieve deferral of income taxes earned by the IBC due to the anti-deferral regimes of the IRS, such as the Passive Foreign Income Corporation (PFIC) and the Controlled Foreign Corporation (CFC) rules. These require US shareholders to report all IBC worldwide income when earned, EVEN if the IBC does not make a distribution to its US shareholders. Always ensure you are aware of and fully understand the tax obligations to which you, as a US person, are subject.

What are bearer shares?

While there are no longer "numbered accounts" which allow true anonymity, there are **bearer shares**, which allow you to come close. A bearer share is a share of stock that belongs to whomever holds (bears) it. There is no identifying information on the shares, so the beneficial owner of an IBC, for instance, can have complete privacy. Panama is one of the countries that allow a company's shareholders to remain anonymous by using this type of share.

Such corporations can even own a bank account completely anonymously, since the ownership of their company is also anonymous.

Things to remember:

- An LLC offers limited liability for all of its members.

- LLCs are ideal for housing high-risk properties, intellectual property, real estate and equipment. The last three can be licensed and/or leased back to your operating company.

- You want to be in a jurisdiction that only affords creditors charging order protection against LLCs. Currently, there are only eight states that offer this as the sole remedy.

- An FLP can reduce tax liability by shifting income to its limited partners in lower tax brackets (children and grandchildren over 14 years of age).

- Bearer shares have no identifying information on them and whoever holds them owns them. Therefore, if a company is owned through bearer shares, its shareholders can remain anonymous but it must report all income and file informational returns identifying shareholders to the IRS.

CHAPTER 6

Who Benefits Most from Asset Preservation Planning?

I cannot afford to waste my time making money. ~Louis Agassiz

The answer is anyone who has anything to lose.

- Professionals (especially those in high-risk professions)

- Business owners

- Anyone who has acquired substantial wealth, or is currently acquiring wealth

- Anyone at risk for lawsuits or claims against their assets

Consider the following examples of different groups of professionals who would greatly benefit from launching an asset protection plan:

Physicians

Many physicians work as much as 80 to 90 hours each week to maintain their clinical practices and see hospital patients. This does not even include on-call time. Physicians invest huge amounts of time and energy in their practices and their patients. As a result, they may believe that taking critical moments away from their work for personal financial planning may result in missed opportunities for financial gain.

Therefore, many physicians postpone this critical step in building wealth and protecting assets. As a result of rapidly soaring medical malpractice insurance costs, physicians are working harder than ever to pay school loans, insurance premiums, and practice debts. Neither can they expect these costs to remain constant. In fact, these expenses continue to increase at alarming rates. Each year, a physician faces the threat that his or her insurance company will raise malpractice premiums by 10, 20, or even 60 percent. In addition to raising insurance premiums, companies keep lowering the caps — the amount of money the policy pays out in the event of a claim.

Consider that a medical malpractice insurance policy typically costs between $130,000 and $160,000 annually. Furthermore, most insurance companies currently limit policies to cover no more than one million dollars per claim. Juries almost never limit their awards to a dollar amount that small. As I said before, the average jury award in malpractice cases was $4.7 million as of 2005.

Recently, a news story posted on the Internet divulged the amount of a claim against a physician practicing in the state of New York. The jury awarded that plaintiff more than $80 million. Additionally, a trauma center based in Las Vegas was forced to cease operating altogether because their physician employees could not obtain affordable medical malpractice insurance.

This phenomenon is prevalent among primary care practitioners. Many family physicians are retiring early or relocating practices due to rising costs. Many newly licensed doctors are opting for more lucrative specialty areas rather than family practice. Despite the rising shortage of doctors, physicians are unable to raise rates to compensate because of insurance and Medicare limitations. Therefore, they are working harder than ever to build wealth.

Protect what you have worked so hard for. Get an asset protection plan in place to safeguard your hard earned wealth and assets today.

Commercial Property Owners and Landlords

Do you own a piece of commercial property? If so, do you rent it out to other individuals who maintain a business operation in that location? If you rent commercial property to one or more tenants, you could very well be perceived by potential litigants as a "landlord with deep pockets." The court dockets today are filled with cases filed against property owners.

In some situations, these landlords are fortunate enough to possess liability insurance policies that are large enough and comprehensive enough to cover any claims made against the property owner. All too often, however, this is not the case. In some cases, a jury will determine that the plaintiff is entitled to a dollar amount that far exceeds the scope of any insurance liability policy currently in effect. If you fall victim to this type of award, the plaintiff's attorney may be able to file a claim against your personal assets. You may, however, legally be able to avoid seizure of your assets if you develop an asset protection plan *before* any claims arise.

Small Business Owners

According to the United States Small Business Administration, a small business is defined as any company that employs less than 500 workers. By this definition, the majority of American business enterprises can be classified as "small." Recently released U.S. government statistics indicate that small businesses located throughout the country employ more than 60 million people. This number represents fifty percent of the American workforce — fully half of all employed persons in the United States work for small businesses.

In fact, some economists and business specialists argue that, if viewed as a separate economic entity, small businesses operating in the United States would comprise the world's third largest economic workforce. The financial impact created by small businesses operating in this country is surpassed only by the overall economies of the U.S and Japan. As a result, small businesses and corporations have ample opportunity to engage in free enterprise — the competitive marketing of their services and products. This also means, however, that there are plenty of opportunities to file lawsuits against those small business owners. Statistically, **one in three** business owners is likely to be sued in any given year.

Owning and operating a small business is hard work. For this reason, many small business owners feel that they are already so overworked that they have no time to worry about making financial plans. Additionally, because most business owners are heavily invested in their businesses, they fail to separate their personal finances from their business finances by incorporating or employing one of the limited liability structures. The end result is that many business owners lose both their business and their personal assets when their companies are sued. Do not make this costly mistake with your finances — initiate an asset protection plan today.

Certified Professional Accountants

Most laypersons tend to perceive the accounting occupation as primarily a low profile profession: account-ants enter the office each day, balance columns of figures, and spend their break times poring over the latest tax code information released by the Internal Revenue Service. At the end of each day, they put away their pens and calculators, shut off their computers, and leave the office, leaving all of their work concerns and worries behind. Certainly, on the surface, their jobs appear to be routine, if not boring.

What most people do not realize is that certified professional accountants, or CPAs, also face significant risk for being named as the defendants in litigation proceedings. In recent months, a popular Internet news site featured a headline revealing that statistics predict **one in ten** CPAs will be sued during any given fiscal year. This risk increases exponentially for accountants who own their own firms.

Unfortunately, many CPAs make the mistake of attempting to focus on other people's financial problems and investments while ignoring or neglecting their own financial planning concerns. Physicians, however, are not the only professionals who are victimized by juries who award damages in excess of $100 million or more. This same fate can befall a CPA. So, before you neglect your own finances, take time to plan carefully and protect your personal assets.

Engineers

Many engineers find it hard to believe that anyone would ever consider suing them. After all, what would be the motivation? As with any other lawsuit, the case is filed because someone wants to obtain money.

Engineers often take little account of this, believing that they are already fully covered and protected by the company for which they work. This may or may not be true, depending on the terms of their company's insurance policy and its exclusions. The actual protection offered the employee may be little or none under a given set of circumstances and the engineer would do well to have an asset protection plan of his own in place before any claims arise.

If you happen to be an engineer who engages in architectural design, you may have additional cause for concern. Increasing numbers of legal claims are being filed in court against engineers. These claims, alleging that the engineers involved are to blame for to faulty structural designs, are often expensive to litigate and settle. Consider, for example, that the hourly fee charged by an expert witness can be in excess of $400!

Just doing your job each day and managing business concerns can be stressful enough. Don't delay. Discuss asset protection strategies with trusted advisors and take this critical step today.

Things to remember:

- Physicians, especially those in high-risk specialties, benefit from asset protection (AP) planning due to increasing malpractice costs and soaring litigation risks.

- Landlords benefit from AP planning due to the prevalence of frivolous and malicious lawsuits against "deep pockets." You'd be surprised how little it takes to slip and fall and how much it can cost you.

- One in three small business owners is sued each year. Small business owners cannot afford **not** to engage in AP planning.

- CPAs are also at risk. One in ten will be sued this year. And the verdicts will not be small. The risk of being sued is even higher if you own your own business. The time to plan is now.

- Engineers need independent asset protection strategies, as their firms may easily not cover them for any litigation that arises.

- Anyone of any means needs an asset protection plan.

CHAPTER 7

Frequently Asked Questions

1. Once I put my money in an offshore asset protection trust, can I get it back?

Yes, you can. As a beneficiary, you can request a distribution of funds. Of course, this is totally discretionary with the trustee, and if he finds that you are under any duress to make this request, then to protect you, he will not honor it under the terms of the trust.

You may also be able to take out a loan using the trust assets as collateral. But, don't forget that you have further protected your trust with a spendthrift clause prohibiting you from pledging your interest in the trust to a creditor.

2. Do I have to report what I make offshore to the U.S. government?

Yes. Every U.S. citizen and green card holder must report worldwide income, i.e., income derived from anywhere in the world, to the IRS.

3. What is the difference between a directed trust and a delegated trust?

In a **directed trust**, the grantor appoints one or more advisors/fiduciaries to handle the investments in the trust, while the trustee is only responsible for its administrative duties.

In a **delegated trust**, it is the trustee, not the grantor, who delegates the investment duties to one or more advisors, and the trustee remains liable in varying degrees for their performance.

4. What is an ETF?

It is an Exchange Traded Fund. It includes currencies. There are seven currently available on the NY Stock Exchange. Going offshore opens up your opportunities to trade in more currencies and funds than you would be able to trade through U.S. markets alone.

5. What is a Double Tax Treaty?

This is where two countries agree to divide up taxing rights to different sources of income. Generally, the source country (where the income is earned) has priority taxing rights and the residence country agrees not to tax that income, usually by giving credit for foreign taxes paid on domestic taxes owed. You can find recent U.S. treaties on the Internet at www.irs.gov.

6. What happens when I cash a check or make a deposit for $10,000 or more in the U.S.?

The U.S. Treasury's Financial Crimes Enforcement Network (FinCEN), consisting of 165 law enforcement agencies, including the FBI and Secret Service, are notified electronically by the U.S. bank.

7. What does protecting assets actually involve?

Protecting assets means insulating assets from creditors and lawsuits. Asset protection is, in short, a matter of being responsible with your wealth. If you do not develop an asset protection plan to safeguard the money you have earned, you may lose it all overnight. A careless business decision, a traffic accident, or even a frivolous lawsuit may deprive you and your family of all the money you have earned throughout your professional career. If you are like most professionals, you will take a few moments to stop and realize just how easy, painless, and important protecting your wealth can be. Then you will be ready to invest all of the time and energy necessary to accomplish this process as quickly as you can arrange to do so.

8. Why should I fear a lawsuit? I am a conscientious professional who works hard to do my job.

Unfortunately, American society has become one in which litigation has become a popular way to become wealthy. This wealth is gained by plaintiffs, who file legal actions, as well as by the attorneys who represent them. Just read the daily newspaper or watch the evening news on television. Chances are high that you will hear about a lawsuit that has just been filed. Most likely, the defendant named in the suit is a professional individual or business service. These plaintiff attorneys often operate on a contingency fee basis by which they collect 25 to 40 percent or more of the assets they recover for their clients through these lawsuits. This type of gain provides a huge incentive for them to secure the highest possible recovery in a lawsuit.

Many wealthy individuals rank fear of a lawsuit as one of their greatest financial concerns, and with good reason. As a result, many of them take the necessary steps to put those fears to rest by engaging in adequate asset protection. Like them, you too can take positive steps to make those fears go away forever!

9. How can I legally avoid the threat of a lawsuit and protect both my business and personal finances?

You can protect yourself and your business from the threat of financial disaster by consulting a qualified asset protection specialist for assistance with asset protection planning. He will advise you how you can most effectively protect your assets from seizure by creditors to satisfy a legal claim. The process of asset planning may seem daunting. However, as long as you have competent advisors on your side helping you every step of the way, it can be done quickly, legally, and much less painfully than you could ever hope.

10. What do you mean by appropriate asset protection planning?

The process of appropriate asset protection planning involves the use of practical and sophisticated business and estate planning tactics such as the use of asset protection trusts and limited liability companies. These strategies will put your assets legally beyond the reach of money-hungry claimants who want to get rich quickly by suing you. Our firm works to transfer and protect your assets using financially sound, legal methods that will safeguard and preserve your wealth.

11. Does asset protection planning involve "hiding" assets or opening secret bank accounts?

Absolutely not! Our firm uses only legal, ethical methods to preserve your wealth. This system is entirely legitimate and uses proven planning techniques that operate entirely according to state and federal law. In addition to your U.S. holdings, you are required to report your worldwide income to the IRS. We carefully follow every Internal Revenue Service rule and regulation. Our planning process is guaranteed.

12. Why don't I simply hide my assets in a Swiss bank account? Wouldn't that protect my assets and preserve my wealth beyond the reach of creditors?

No! Depositing funds in any foreign account, even a Swiss bank account, is never 100 percent secure. Realize that there is no such thing as a numbered account anymore, so no more secret bank accounts. (See, Bearer Shares, chapters two and five, for more information to legally remain anonymous.) Also, no investment, whether foreign or domestic, is ever completely guaranteed. Making a foreign investment without a qualified advisor is a possible route to creating a financial disaster.

Simply put, hiding your money in this way is illegal. Prudent asset protection planning is not a tax avoidance device. If you try to engage in a form of asset protection planning by hiding assets like this, you will encounter serious penalties. Each taxpayer is legally required to report every investment or bank account in which he or she has a financial interest. This requirement includes, but is not limited to, signature authority and foreign bank or investment accounts.

And, when a judgment is issued against you, the court can order you to return all of these funds to the United States. This will make those offshore funds available for satisfying creditor claims. If you choose to disobey the court and keep these assets hidden, you will be in violation of federal laws. Then, you risk severe financial consequences and even incarceration.

13. I gifted all of my assets to my spouse, so I have nothing to worry about, right?

Wrong! This is, at best, a temporary solution to your problems. If you take this action, you lose control over your own assets. This is especially true in the event of a divorce or separation from your spouse. In addition, your spouse may be sued for personal or professional reasons and lose the lawsuit. In this event, all of your assets are at risk.

Even if your spouse is not sued, consider the consequences that may occur if you do have outstanding judgments against you that cannot be collected and your spouse dies. Suddenly, all the assets and money that were placed in her name become yours. Your creditors can now seize those assets. Overnight, you are faced with the partial or total loss of all of your assets and property. There will be nothing you can to do prevent this from occurring.

14. We carry a huge multi-million dollar liability insurance policy, so aren't our assets secure?

Definitely not! This kind of thinking is very dangerous. Remember, none of the liability policies currently in effect insure their holders against intentional wrongdoing. Nor do they provide coverage for the payment of punitive damages. Many litigants request that the defendant pay punitive damages to additionally compensate them for negligence or liability. Further, you may be sued for an amount that far exceeds the limit of your liability policy. Insurance companies have also been known to go out of business, which would leave you with no financial protection and a useless piece of paper.

Liability policies are important, and are often an essential component of an asset protection plan, but they will not offer you complete financial security and protection. Furthermore, if you do maintain a comprehensive strategy for safeguarding your assets, you may receive a significant discount on the cost of your insurance policy. Frequently, the discount realized will easily cover the cost of creating and maintaining an asset protection plan. Keep in mind this important fact, as well: *Some clients have saved thousands or even tens of thousands of dollars per year in liability and malpractice insurance because, once our asset protection system is in place, their liability insurance requirements are often lower.*

It is important to understand that no insurance policy will effectively protect you if you *personally* guarantee a business loan and that business fails. Insurance will not protect you in the event that you are accused of gross negligence or recklessness. And it will never protect you beyond the maximum limits of your coverage.

15. I have a living trust, so my assets are secure, correct?

No. this is not correct. A revocable living trust, when properly structured, is definitely a necessary component in proper estate planning. The trust will allow the assets transferred into it to avoid probate court. A living trust, however, will not protect you from having your assets seized by creditors. If you lose a lawsuit, the court can and often will issue an order to revoke the trust agreement and use those funds to pay the creditor.

16. Is it true that if I protect my assets I can lower my risk of being sued?

You do indeed face a lower risk of being sued with an AP plan in place. Many people mistakenly believe that insurance coverage and liability policies are the best methods of protecting themselves against a lawsuit. Unfortunately this is not true. In fact, creditors who know that you have insurance coverage are *more* likely to file lawsuits against you. This is because they know that you have "deep pockets" and can pay them a lot of money if they win the lawsuit.

On the other hand, if you have your assets properly protected, creditors will be deterred from filing a lawsuit against you in the first place. When a lawyer examines your case and sees that the chances of collecting are slim, even if the court does grant a judgment in his favor, he may not accept the case. This is because most plaintiff attorneys work on a contingency fee basis. If they collect on the judgment, their fee is paid. No collection = no fee = no case. If you protect your assets properly, you will become an unattractive defendant.

17. What constitutes asset protection? Is it the best route to go? If so, why doesn't everybody protect his or her assets in this manner?

Unfortunately, not everyone knows how to do this or is even aware of how important it is. You can protect assets from creditors and lawsuits using a variety of different strategies and techniques. If you use an OAPT, the money in the trust is protected because it is subject to another country's laws. These laws may make it virtually impossible to collect debts or successfully sue the beneficiary except under limited circumstances.

Any creditor who wants to attempt to seize the assets protected by the trust may well have to hire a lawyer in the country in which the trust is established (note that it is often illegal in these countries for an attorney to work on a contingency fee basis). The creditor would then have to convince the court in the country in which the trust is located that it has authority or jurisdiction to even hear the case. This is often quite difficult because foreign countries with favorable APT legislation rarely accept jurisdiction for cases against individual debtors to be satisfied with trust assets. You, the individual settlor, and beneficiary, are distinct legal entities from the trust.

Even if the creditor somehow succeeds in this attempt and the case proceeds, the person who filed the lawsuit will still have to prove that the laws that forbid that court from awarding any of the money in the trust do not apply to him. This is difficult to achieve, if not impossible. For this reason, few people will even bother to try. Almost everyone will simply try to go after someone else instead, and will be happy to accept even the smallest settlement offer.

Generally, the only instance in which an offshore trust can fail to protect assets occurs when the beneficiary waits to set up the trust until after someone is already going after his or her money. That is why early asset protection planning is so critical. As long as the trust is set up well in advance of any such dispute, the trust's assets will be protected.

18. Will someone else control my money?

No. You stay in control of your money at all times by appointing friendly advisors to the trust to instruct the trustee. You have absolute power to remove and replace trustees, with or without cause.

19. Are there any tax consequences to this arrangement?

If structured properly, you can achieve income, estate and gift tax neutrality.

20. Can asset protection ever be considered illegal?

As long as the plan is instituted before any legal situation arises, it is completely legal. Once creditors are after you and a suit has been filed, however, it may become more difficult to protect your assets at that stage. That is why it is prudent to act now and to take positive steps to protect your assets *before* something happens.

21. Where will my assets be located?

The assets themselves may be deposited anywhere. If you prefer, you can keep them exactly where they are this minute, even if they are deposited in your local bank. Only the trust structure itself must be domiciled in an offshore nation. (Still, it is ideal for the assets to be located offshore as well) Work with your planner to select a country with a sound economic environment, favorable laws and an adequate number of trustees available. Modern methods of communication and a stable political arena are also vital to the safety of your money. Our firm works hard to fully investigate all options and to ensure that our clients' funds are domiciled in the best possible location.

22. I am currently being sued. Is it too late to protect my assets?

As we stated earlier, advanced planning is always most effective. We can offer you the best protection by structuring your plan long before creditors are on your heels. However, we have still been able to help many clients even after litigation has begun, subject to federal, state, and foreign fraudulent conveyance statutes. Try not to panic, and seek immediate assistance from competent professionals such as ourselves. We will act as expediently as possible to protect you as best we can under the circumstances. You have nothing to lose by trying to properly protect your assets, and everything to lose by doing nothing.

Glossary

Actual Intent: shown by circumstantial evidence, through "badges of fraud"(see below) that a transfer into an asset protection structure was made with actual intent to hinder, delay, or defraud any creditor.

Anti-Duress Clause: term in a trust contract that directs the trustee to ignore requests for disbursement made by the beneficiary when he is under duress, such as an order by a U.S. court to repatriate funds.

Asset Protection Trust (APT): a trust set up for the purpose of protecting assets from creditors.

Badges of Fraud: points which demonstrate or imply that a debtor had actual intent to hinder, delay, or defraud any creditor.

Bearer Shares: corporate shares with no recorded owner. Whoever holds them, owns them.

Beneficiary: the person or entity who is designated to reap the benefits of the trust.

Civil Law Jurisdictions: jurisdictions where the laws are codified and the principal basis of law is statutory.

Common Law Jurisdictions: jurisdictions that have inherited English law.

Common Stock: common shares of a corporation that provide the holder the potential for capital gains and dividends as well as giving him one vote for each common share.

Constructive Fraud: objective test as to whether a debtor's transfer into an asset protection structure was to hinder, delay or defraud any creditor.

Corporation: a legal entity owned by its shareholders, who elect its officers and directors. It must keep numerous formalities, including holding regular meetings and taking minutes.

Directed Trust: trust that is managed administratively by the trustee while the assets are managed by another person or entity appointed by the settlor/grantor.

Distribution Advisor: party to a directed trust contract, who oversees the trustee's distribution of funds.

Delegated Trust: trust that is managed by the trustee while the assets are managed by another person or entity to whom this duty is delegated by the trustee.

Domestic Asset Protection Trust (DAPT): an asset protection trust organized under the laws of one of the 50 United States or D.C.

Duress Clause: term in a trust contract that directs the trustee to ignore requests for disbursement made by the beneficiary when under duress, such as an order by a U.S. court to repatriate funds.

Family Limited Partnership (FLP): a limited partnership structure used in asset protection planning. Typically involves parents, children and/or grandchildren.

Flee Clause: a clause in a trust contract that directs the trustee to move the trust and change the governing law when facing an attack on the trust.

Foreign Asset Protection Trust (FAPT): an asset protection trust set up under the laws of a foreign jurisdiction.

Fraudulent Conveyance: any transfer made with the intent to hinder, delay, or defraud any creditor (must show actual intent or constructive fraud).

Fraudulent Transfer: any transfer made with the intent to hinder, delay, or defraud any creditor (must show actual intent or constructive fraud).

Grantor: the party to the trust contract who transfers assets into the trust.

Homestead Exemption: exempts some or all of the equity in your home from creditor attack. The amount exempted depends on the laws of your state.

International Business Corporation (IBC): legal business entity established in a foreign country for the purpose of doing business elsewhere. Has few reporting obligations and pays no income tax on profits.

Limited Liability Company (LLC): limited liability asset protection structure in which no member has general liability.

Limited Partnership (LC): must have at least one general partner and one limited partner. The general partner has unlimited liability for partnership debts but all the management rights. The limited partner has no management rights and his liability is limited to his share in the business.

Offshore Asset Protection Trust (OAPT): an asset protection trust set up under the laws of a foreign jurisdiction.

Rule Against Perpetuities: rule that applies to future dispositions of property, which states that trusts, wills, etc., cannot endure for more than 21 years beyond the death of the last beneficiary who was alive at the time of the trust's creation.

S Corporation: a corporation that can consist of no more than 75 shareholders, with "pass-through" taxation. Shareholders are taxed as individuals; the corporation isn't taxed. Only U.S. persons are permitted as shareholders.

Self-Settled Trust: one where the grantor is also the only beneficiary.

Series LLCs: one large LLC with several cells. Each cell or "series" has its own book of accounts and is treated as a separate entity, but only the parent LLC is required to be registered.

Settlor: the party to the trust contract who transfers assets into the trust.

Spendthrift Clause: a clause in a trust contract that provides that a beneficiary cannot pledge his expectancy in trust assets to a creditor. If he does, the trustee is directed by the trust documents not to pay it.

Statute of Elizabeth: originally enacted in England in 1571 during the reign of Elizabeth I, this statute was the progenitor of modern fraudulent conveyance rules. It still exists in varying forms in many offshore common law jurisdictions.

Tax Haven: traditionally a jurisdiction where you pay little or no taxes on your earnings.

Trust: a legal entity formed by a contract between a grantor (or settlor), trustee and beneficiaries. Sometimes there can be additional parties: distribution advisors or trust protectors.

Trustee: the party to the trust contract who is given legal title to the trust assets and is then charged with managing the trust for the benefit of the beneficiaries, according to the grantor's expressed wishes.

Trust Protector: a party to a trust contract who protects the grantor's interests by, among other things, watching over the trustee to ensure he does his job properly.

Index

1-9

401(k), 9

A

Accounting, 7
Actual Intent, 15, 17
Agassiz, Louis, 61
Alabama, 50, 55
Alaska, 31–32, 37, 55
Alaska Trust Act, 37–41
Anderson, Michael and
    Denyse, 14, 17
Anguilla, 57
Antigua, 57
Arizona, 55
Arkansas, 50
Asset Protection Planning, *see*
    Chapter 1
Asset Protection Trusts, what
    they are, 12
Assets, what to protect, 10

Assets, when to protect, 11
Austria, 46

B

Badges of fraud, 15–16
Bahamas, the, 28, 46, 57
Bankruptcy Code, 15
Bearer shares, 59
Belize, 46, 57
Beneficiaries, 12
Bermuda, 46
British Virgin Islands, 46–47, 57
Business, high-risk, 7

C

Cayman Islands, the, 46–47
Certificates of deposit (CDs), 23
Certified professional accoun-
    tants, liability, 65
Civil law jurisdictions, 27
Colorado, 50

Commercial Property,
    liability, 63
Common law jurisdictions, 26
Constructive Fraud, 16
Controlled Foreign Corp
    (CFC), 58
Cook Islands, 14, 17, 27, 28,
    46–47
Corporations, C and S, 12, 21
Current accounts, 23

D

DAPT, 12, 14, 31
DAPT, weaknesses of, 45
Decanting, Reformation and
    Modification Statute, 34
Delaware, 31–34, 41–44, 50, 55
Delaware Qualified
    Dispositions in Trust Act,
    35, 41
Denmark, 46
Deposit accounts, 23
Distributions, 13
District of Columbia, 50
Domestic Asset Protection
    Trust, see DAPT,
Double tax treaty, 70
Duress clause, 17, 20

E

Engineers, liability, 65
ERISA qualified retirement
    plans, 9
Exchange Traded Fund (ETF),
    70

F

Family Limited Partnership
    (FLP), 12, 33, 56, 59
FDIC, 35
Federal Trade Commission,
    14
Fiduciary accounts, 23
Financial account, definition
    of, 25
Financial Crimes Enforcement
    Network (FinCEN), 70
Financial institution,
    definition of, 26
Flee clause, 20, 27
Florida, 50, 55
Foreign financial institution,
    definition of, 26
Franklin, Benjamin, 31
Fraud, 14
Fraudulent transfer rules, 11,
    13, 15–17, 28, 42

G

Georgia, 50
Gibraltar, 28, 46, 57
Grantor, 12, 20
Guernsey, 46

H

HIRE Act, 24–26, 30, 45, 47
Homestead Exemption, 9
Hong Kong, 29, 46

I

Idaho, 50
International Business
   Corporations (IBC), 12,
   57–59
Investment accounts, 23
IRA, 9
IRS, 22, 29, 32, 58, 59
Isle of Man, 46–47

J

Jersey, 46

K

Kansas, 50

L

Lawrence, Stephen J., 17–18
Liability insurance, 11
Liability, AMA study, 8
Liability, high risk businesses,
   7, 62
Liechtenstein, 27, 45–47
Limited Liability Company
   (LLC), 12, 14, 15, 33, 53–56,
   59
Limited Partnership (LP), 12,
   33
Living trust, revocable, 75
Luxembourg, 27

M

Maine, 50

Malpractice, medical, 8
Managed accounts, 23
Medicine, 7
Missouri, 50
Murphy, 32

N

Nebraska, 50
Nevada, 32
Nevis, 46, 57
New Hampshire, 50
New Mexico, 50
NJSA, 50
Non-judicial settlement
   agreements, *see NJSA*
North Carolina, 50
North Dakota, 55

O

OAPT, 12, 20–30
OFC Report, 29
Office of the Comptroller of
   the Currency (OCC), 35
Office of Thrift Supervision
   (OTS), 35
Offshore Asset Protection
   Trust, *see OAPT*
Offshore Bank Accounts, 22–30
Offshore Planning, *see
   Chapter 2*
Ohio, 50
Oklahoma, 50
Oregon, 50

P

Panama, 27, 29, 46–47, 57
Passive Foreign Income Corp
    (PFIC), 58
Passthru payment, 25
Pennsylvania, 50
Physician Insurers Association
    of America, 8
Ponzi schemes, 14, 17
Precious metals accounts, 23
Protectors, *see Trust
    Protectors*

Q

Qualified dispositions, 35, 43
Qualified trustee, 43

R

Recalcitrant account holder, 25
Retirement plans, 9
Roosevelt, Franklin Delano, 7
Roth IRA, 9

S

Safekeeping accounts, 23
Samoa, 47
Settlor, 12
Seychelles Islands, 57
Singapore, 46–47
Situs, *see Chapter 3*
Small business owners,
    liability, 64
South Carolina, 50
South Dakota, 31–37, 47, 49, 55

South Dakota Self-Settled
    Trust Statute, 35
St. Vincent, 47
Statute of Elizabeth, 26–27
Steinem, Gloria, 49
Structuring, 23
Switzerland, 27, 29, 46

T

Tax haven, 28–29
Tennessee, 50
Texas, 50 55
Trust Protectors, 20, 36
Trustee, 12, 29–30
Trusts, delegated, 69
Trusts, directed, 21, 34, 49–51,
    69
Trusts, dynasty, 27, 32
Trusts, irrevocable, 13
Trusts, self-settled, 13, 17, 20
Trusts, spendthrift clause, 13
Turks & Caicos Islands, 46
Twin accounts, 23

U

UK territories, 47
Umbrella policy, 11
Uniform Fraudulent
    Conveyance Act (UFCA),
    15
Uniform Fraudulent Transfers
    Act (UFTA), 15
Uniform Trust Code, 50
United States Account,
    definition of, 25

United States foreign entity,
    definition of, 26
US Customs and Border
    Protection Agency, 22–23
US Treasury Department, 58
Utah, 50

V

Virginia, 50, 55

W

Withholdable payment, 25
Wyoming, 50

CPSIA information can be obtained at www.ICGtesting.com
Printed in the USA
LVOW010727171011

250760LV00001B/3/P